The Little Book of
MANAGEMENT
BOLLOCKS

WH

C

AL

POCKET BOOKS

First published in Great Britain by Pocket Books, 2001
An imprint of Simon & Schuster UK Ltd
A Viacom Company

1 3 5 7 9 10 8 6 4 2

Simon & Schuster UK Ltd
Africa House · 64-78 Kingsway · London WC2B 6AH

Simon & Schuster Australia · Sydney

A CIP catalogue record for this book is available from the British Library

ISBN 0-7434-0413-0

Designed by Lovelock & Co.
Printed and bound in Great Britain by William Clowes Ltd

MISSION STATEMENT

This book is dedicated to helping the reader achieve the ultimate management goal of becoming rich, successful, dynamic, unpleasant, and utterly incomprehensible.

And God said, Let there be light: and there was light. And God saw the light, that it was good: and God divided the light from the darkness. And God called the light Day, and the darkness he called Management. And God said, Let there be best value performance indicators, that all the beasts of the field may compete in a global marketplace. And Lo, the earth brought forth beasts of the field and creeping things, which were promoted unto senior management positions and given dominion over all mankind. And on the Seventh Day, God rested, and said unto Himself, 'I wonder if I should have outsourced this to someone who knew what they were doing?'

CORE COMPETENCIES

Your organisation's core competencies must be protected at all costs. If you're not sure whether your organisation has any core competencies left, bring in outside consultants.
(To pay for the outside consultants, it may be necessary to close down your core competencies.)

STRESS MANAGEMENT
1

Watch out for signs of stress and do something about it before it's too late. Early stress warning signals include:

- Apathy.
- Headaches.
- Irritability.
- Loss of concentration.
- Throwing yourself off high buildings.

NEGATIVE OUTCOMES

A negative outcome is not a failure;
it is a learning opportunity.
An extreme negative outcome
is a *massive* learning opportunity.
Be proud – people are learning
so much from you!

ENABLERS

Don't just be an enabler, be a proactive, innovative, and risk-taking enabler! Explain to your team that in a project-driven matrix organisation, where organisational sub-systems provide enhanced double-loop learning paradigms, the challenging of structural assumptions is as inherent to strategic planning as an enhanced implementation analysis is to forward visionary thinking.

Illustrate this point by asking everyone to work over the weekend.

FEEDBACK

Get feedback from your staff as to what
kind of leader you are.
Take subordinates aside and ask
them frankly:
How do I come across?
Do I command respect?
Do I communicate well?
Do I take good decisions?
Do you want to keep your job?

FAMILY LIFE

Reinvigorate your family life by importing positive management models into the home:

Introduce total quality
management into mowing the lawn.
Implement key performance
indicators for the cleaning lady.
Write a mission statement for
the milkman.
Outsource your children.
Downsize your spouse.
Re-engineer the cat.

ASSETS

Your most precious asset is *you.*
Take care of your asset.
Give your asset a comfortable office.
Let your asset take long holidays.
Award your asset a pay-rise.
If anyone complains, tell them
to kiss your asset.

UNDERPERFORMING

Dealing with under-performers requires
a high level of emotional intelligence.
Having analysed the nature of the
performance shortfall, ask the individual
concerned to suggest solutions.
Listen carefully. Show empathy.
Clarify expectations.
Ask open-ended, non-directive questions.
Make sympathetic, non-prescriptive,
non-judgmental remarks.
Then replace the fucker with someone
who can do the job.

EFFECTIVE COMMUNICATION

Ensure effective inter-personal communication among your staff by providing comfortable areas or corners where employees can meet and chat on an informal basis.

(NB. Make sure the concealed microphones are working.)

NEWCOMERS

Integrate new employees by making sure they understand your corporate vision, your sense of mission, your core values, and your own personal need for blind, unquestioning obedience.

PERFORMANCE REVIEWS

The annual performance review can be an arduous experience for many people. Empower your staff by inviting them to estimate their own cash value to the organization.
(Test their self-confidence by pretending you think the sum mentioned is in pesetas.)

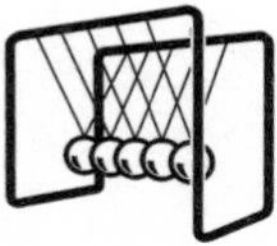

MOTIVATION
#1

It is often assumed that money is
the only motivational factor.
Wrong.
Fear is also important.
Save money. Use fear.

A BAD MANAGER SAYS:

Eleanor, I want you to do two people's jobs.

A GOOD MANAGER SAYS:

Eleanor, you're a natural multi-tasker.

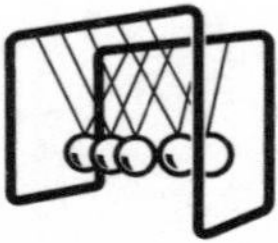

A BAD MANAGER SAYS:

You know nothing.

A GOOD MANAGER SAYS:

We're inviting you to attend a seminar on problem-solving and ongoing improvement strategies.

A BAD MANAGER SAYS:

I'm sorry. You'll have to work
all the hours God sends.

A GOOD MANAGER SAYS:

I'm proud. This is a 24/7 organisation.

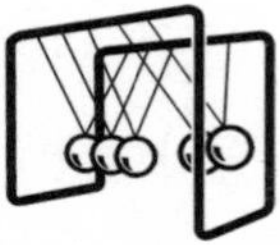

A BAD MANAGER SAYS:

How come no one tells me anything?

A GOOD MANAGER SAYS:

To counter information deficit syndrome,
I'm actioning increased interactive feedback.

A BAD MANAGER SAYS:

How the hell are we going to get *that* past the morons on the board?

A GOOD MANAGER SAYS:

Our experiential curve suggests that this initiative will face internal structural constraints.

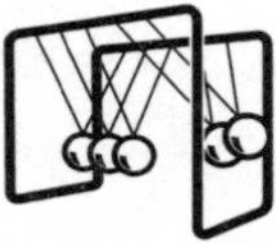

A BAD MANAGER SAYS:

We screwed up.

A GOOD MANAGER SAYS:

Some recent corporate strategies have had a high negative impact outcome.

THE IMPORTANCE OF HUMOUR #1

Humour is an under-used tool. Impress other people by taking out your under-used tool at unexpected moments.

If other people don't like your under-used tool, put it away quickly.

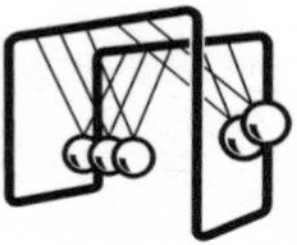

CHALLENGE ASSUMPTIONS

Challenge popular conventions in the workplace whenever possible:

- Don't pay anybody's wages.
- Lock all the toilets for a day.
- Switch off the air-conditioning.

Use any adverse employee reaction as a means of identifying non-ambitious personnel.

INFORMATION OVERLOAD

Help employees who are suffering
from information overload
by not telling them anything.

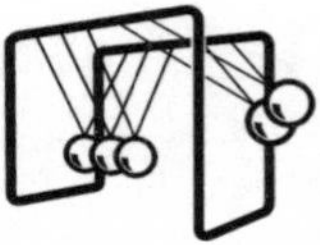

STRESS MANAGEMENT
2

Stress can lead to bouts of self-destructive behaviour. The most common examples of self-destructive behaviour are:

- Smoking
- Drinking
- Over-eating
- Being smarter than your boss

MISTAKES

Colleagues can becomes very upset when their mistakes are criticised. Instead of criticising colleagues for their mistakes, criticise them for their appearance instead. For example, say, 'Good God, John, I'd never realised before just how huge and ugly your nose is.' Once you've said stuff like that a few times, John will be only too happy to be criticised for his mistakes.

NON-VERBAL COMMUNICATION SKILLS

To bring about dramatic improvements in non-verbal communication skills, seal up your subordinates' mouths with masking tape.

HUMAN AND NATURAL

Many natural resources are not renewable.
Conserve natural resources by destroying
human resources instead.

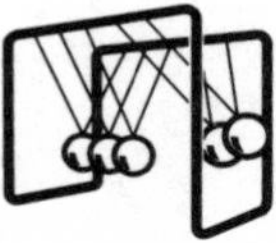

BUILDING ON SUCCESS

Let success become a way of life:

- Be a success at work.
- Be a success in your social activities.
- Be a success in your family life.
- Be a success on the tennis court.
- Be a success in your local community.
- Be a success in your PTA.
- Be a success in your triple heart-bypass support group.

GLOBAL ACCOUNT MANAGEMENT

Simplify your global account management by not counting your own travel expenses.

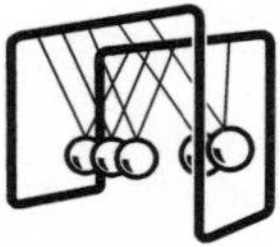

NAMES

Interpersonal communication benefits hugely from the friendly use of first names. Remember, even the most junior member of your team has a first name. If the trainee filing clerk is called Rob, don't just say 'good morning', say 'good morning, Rob'. If Rob screws up on a task, don't say, 'you're an asshole', say, 'you're an asshole, Rob'.

INVESTMENT OUTCOMES

Improve investment outcomes
by never investing.

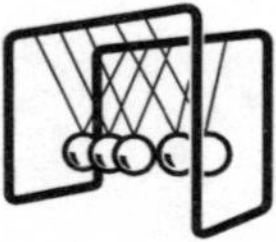

THE KEY

If the key you have chosen does not open
the door, it is not necessarily the wrong key –
it could be the wrong door.
Or it could be the right key and the right
door, only you had too much to drink at
last night's office party.

COUNTING YOUR TRIUMPHS

Feeling there aren't enough triumphs
in your career?
Make figures count for you.
Ten plus ten is twenty.
Ten *times* ten is a hundred.
Don't add up your triumphs, multiply them!
(Divide your mistakes by ten.)

CORPORATE IDENTITY

Your personal identity and your corporate identity can never be separated.

Merge your personal and corporate identities by branding yourself with your company's logo.

(Choose whatever part of your anatomy you consider most appropriate.)

LOYALTY

Impress on your staff the crucial importance of loyalty to their employer.

Test that loyalty by setting off the fire alarm.

Dismiss all those who leave their desks.

APPRAISAL MEETINGS
#1

Put employees at their ease at appraisal meetings by taking off your jacket, loosening your tie, kicking off your shoes, unzipping your pants, and smiling fixedly.

WRONG DECISIONS

Anyone can make a wrong decision
– even you!
Let your staff see you are human by
calling a meeting where you admit
you made a wrong decision.
Ask who is prepared to take responsibility
for your wrong decision.

DELEGATING NOT DUMPING

Learn the difference between
delegating and dumping.
Others dump.
You delegate.

HATS

Avoid blocked thinking by changing hats.
On Monday, wear your manager's hat.
On Tuesday, wear your sales hat.
On Wednesday, wear your teamwork hat.
On Thursday, wear your logistics hat.
On Friday, wear your wife's hat.
See if anybody notices the difference.

THE IMPORTANCE OF HUMOUR # 2

Playfulness and humour are an essential part of being a good manager. When interviewing for a new appointment, ease tension by placing a whoopee cushion on the applicant's chair.

LEADERSHIP

Management is not the same as leadership.
A manager sees a crisis as something to be coped with.
A leader sees a crisis as an opportunity.
If you discover your company is about to go bust, be a leader, not a manager: seize all the cash assets you can lay your hands on and escape abroad.

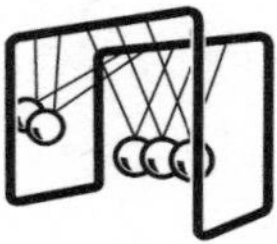

PRESENTATIONS

During presentations it's important to get people nodding and saying 'yes'. You can achieve this by:

- Presenting a fact that's startling but obviously true.
- Identifying a problem everyone has experienced.
- Making a general statement with which no one is likely to disagree.
- Asking if anybody's bored.

WORKING FROM HOME

Others work at home. You work *from* home. After a day or two working from home, take extra care to be an inspirational manager when you return to the office.

If you've accidentally acquired a suntan while working from home, report sick and stay in bed till the tan's gone.

QUESTIONS MANAGERS ASK

Q: What's the best way to criticise my boss?

A: Very, very quietly, so that he can't hear you.

QUESTIONS MANAGERS ASK

Q: What can I do to be more appreciated and accepted by my colleagues?

A: Visit a dental hygienist.

QUESTIONS MANAGERS ASK

Q: What should I do if I find my company is behaving in an illegal or unethical way?

A: Your company never behaves in an illegal or unethical way.

QUESTIONS MANAGERS ASK

Q: Should I socialise with my subordinates?

A: Yes. But make sure nobody comes into the bedroom half-way through.

QUESTIONS MANAGERS ASK

Q: How do I get into the habit of thinking outside the box?

A: Make sure your box is very, very small.

QUESTIONS MANAGERS ASK

Q: How do I awaken the giant within?

A: Get real. Awaken the pygmy instead.

USEFUL ACRONYMS
#1

Benchmarking
Upsizing
Leadership
Loop analysis
Shared values
Honesty
Innovation
Teamworking

OPTIMISM

It is an established fact that optimists sell more, achieve more and make more money than pessimists do.

So always surround yourself with pessimists.

Then, no matter how useless you are, you'll look like a success.

EMPATHY

A good manager displays empathy
for the personal needs of every individual
in the workplace, no matter how
insignificant their role.

Develop your empathy skills
by smiling at slugs.

MEETINGS

People often fail to make contributions during meetings simply because of fear of ridicule. Help team members to overcome their fear of ridicule by only laughing at them behind their backs.

PROGRESS

Not rising through the ranks of management as fast as you would like? Think of yourself as a corporation in need of change and give yourself a corporate-style makeover:

- Redesign yourself.
- Rebrand yourself.
- Reposition yourself.
- Repackage yourself.

If necessary, buy a new pullover.

BRAINSTORMING

Jump-start your contribution to brainstorming sessions by plugging yourself into the mains.

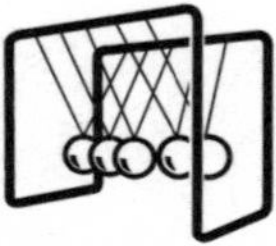

USEFUL ACRONYMS
#2

Willing
Able
Neat
Knowledgeable
Enthusiastic
Resourceful

LOYALTY

Demonstrate your commitment to your employer by staying in the office twenty-four hours a day, seven days a week and communicating with your family by video-conferencing. Maintain healthy relations with your children by sending them e-mails on their birthdays. (Your pc can be programmed to do this automatically.)

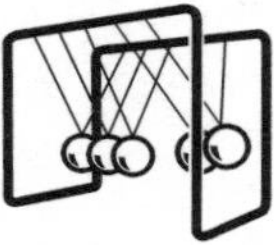

SURFING

Up to 45 per cent of all internet
usage at work is inappropriate.
Wait till subordinates have gone home
then check their computers
to see if they've been downloading
any pornographic material.
If they have, examine the
material thoroughly.
Use the zoom to clarify details.
Take as much time as you need.
Shower afterwards.

DELEGATING

Being a successful manager means knowing when to delegate and knowing when to do something yourself. Look at each problem and decide which response is the appropriate one.

If the problem's a blocked toilet, definitely delegate.

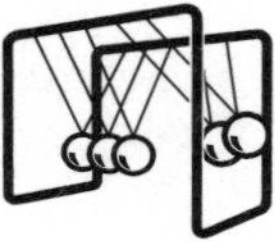

STRETCHING

People work better when they are stretched.
Stretch your team by making them work for
forty-eight hours without a break.
Don't forget to stretch yourself as well.
(Keep a sofa in your office for this purpose).

EXECUTIVE RETREATS

An executive retreat can be one of the most effective investments a corporation will ever make.
Select five or six of your most agreeable colleagues and book yourselves into a luxury hotel for a few days.
Take along an after-dinner facilitator to help you with those confusing corridors.

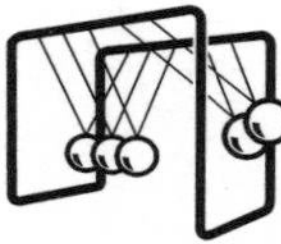

APPRAISAL MEETINGS #2

End appraisal meetings on an optimistic note. As employees leave the room, mention casually that your company's early retirement package is the best in the business.

BLAME

If you're not achieving your aims, don't blame government policy, head office decisions, the state of the economy, the strength of the pound or the high rate of taxation. Instead, have the courage to blame the person who's really responsible – your predecessor.

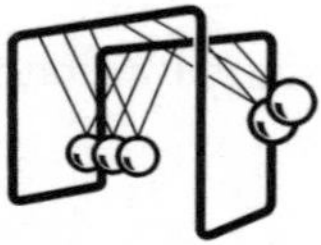

PREJUDICE

When recruiting, don't let personal prejudices interfere with your choice of candidates. Draw up a list of objective recruitment criteria, such as:

Does s/he have a degree in business studies?

Does s/he have management experience?

Does s/he have communicating and negotiating skills?

Is s/he wearing one of those horrid digital watches?

SEXUAL HARASSMENT

Sexual harassment in the workplace is a very grave offence. So make sure you don't get caught. (Practise on someone very junior.)

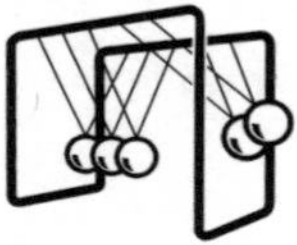

PROMOTION

Promotion is an opportunity.

Don't make the mistake of promoting mediocre people to positions of power simply in order to protect your own position.

Promote mediocre people to positions of power so that you've got someone to talk to.

MANAGING CHANGE

Older employees can sometimes feel threatened by change. Help them adapt to change by appointing a young line manager to supervise and support them. (Why not take the opportunity to do something for the community and offer the job to a youngster just released from detention?)

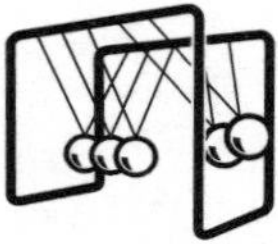

DOWNSIDES

When examining the downside of any proposal, don't be afraid to look clearly and boldly at the worst case scenario.

If the worst case scenario is the loss of your job, it's probably best to look clearly and boldly at someone else's worst case scenario instead.

YOUR POTENTIAL

Your potential is as big as you want it to be. If a senior colleague doubts this, just say, 'I bet my potential's bigger than yours'.

If he wants to argue, draw an outline of your potential on a flip-chart. Don't be afraid to exaggerate a little.

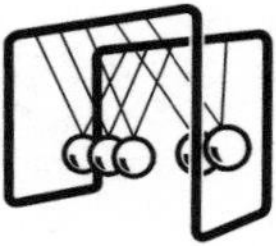

INSPIRING OTHERS

As a manager, it's your job to inspire others.

If there's nothing inspiring about you,
just use fear instead.

BAD IDEAS

If a subordinate comes up with a poorly formulated proposal in a meeting, don't say 'that sucks'.

Instead say, 'that's a very interesting and original concept', then get rid of the creep as soon as possible.

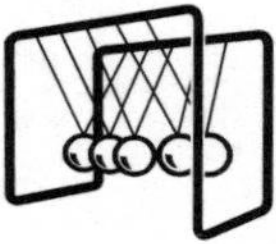

JOB SECURITY

In the modern marketplace, job security is an outmoded concept. Help employees adapt to the modern marketplace by creeping up on them and bursting a balloon behind their backs.
When they jump with fright, laugh and say, 'that wasn't a balloon bursting, that was a metaphor about job security'.
Then walk away chuckling quietly to yourself.

SOCIAL LIFE

The purpose of your social life is
to enhance your career.
Regard every drinks gathering as
a chance to market yourself.
Think of every office outing as a career
enhancement opportunity. See every dinner
party as a self-branding exercise.
Treat every sexual experience as preparation
for when you get fucked by your employer.

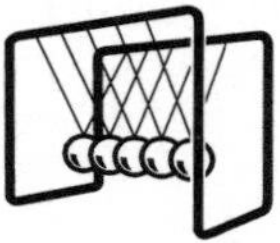

BODY LANGUAGE

During presentations, watch out for signs of inattention in your audience. This could include coughing, shuffling, frowning, doodling, yawning, scratching, sleeping, masturbating, making phone calls, reading books, writing books, taking a bath, getting married, committing suicide. If you see anyone engaged in these activities, it's probably time to start asking questions about your presentational skills.

BENCHMARKING

Benchmarking means analysing the performance of your competitors with a view to improving your own performance. Counteract competitive activity by pinpointing your competitor's weaknesses. Look for vulnerable areas in their field of operation (e.g., an open window through which to throw the firebomb).

TEAM PLAYER

Be a team player.
Crack jokes with the other guys.
Get tickets to a show and invite
them all along.
Go out for a meal with them.
Ask them back to your place for group
sex with your wife and neighbours.

RECRUITMENT

Put candidates at their ease. Show that you value the relaxed approach by falling asleep during interviews.

PERSONAL GLORY

If people congratulate you personally on something that was actually the work of your team, smile and murmur, 'I couldn't have done it without my team'.

Everybody will think you're just being modest.

THE IMPORTANCE OF HUMOUR #3

Bring playfulness and humour into the workplace.

Next time you fire somebody, bring a smile to their face by putting on a red nose just before you break the news.

FAILURE

Failure is a learned response.

Avoid failure by not learning anything.

SELF-REALISATION

Self-realisation through personal
endeavour is the highest pinnacle of
human achievement.
Self-realisation through money
is a close second.

So who needs to come first all the time?

TEAM SPIRIT

Staff who regularly take part in team sports are more likely to co-operate in the workplace. Develop your staff's teamwork skills by encouraging them to take up synchronised swimming. Harness their enthusiasm by calling it *synergised* swimming! Get non-swimmers to take part too.

If anybody drowns, ask the others what they've learnt from the experience.

MOTIVATION
#2

A sophisticated motivational strategy goes beyond mere financial reward. Explain to your team that self-esteem and a sense of personal achievement are more important than money. Better still, get someone else to explain this to them.

MOTIVATIONAL POSTERS

Motivational posters should be striking, simple, and effective. For example:

Failure is only a staging post
on the road to success.

or

Take charge of your job.
Take charge of your life.

or

Good is good,
but excellent is better!

or

Work harder,
you fat-arsed bastards.

WASTEFUL PRACTICES

Get rid of wasteful practices.
Stop paying people.

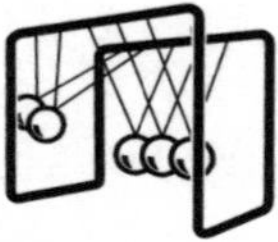

TALKING TRUTH TO POWER

Power needs truth. That's why it's important to give true and accurate information to your superior. Don't shy away from giving a full account of everyday life in the general office. (It may be best to avoid mentioning the incident with the baguettes and the pantyhose.)

SELF-ACTUALISATION

Self-actualisation through personal endeavour is the highest pinnacle of human achievement. Try self-actualising whenever you have a free moment: in your car, on the train, in the bath, on the toilet. (Top managers can ask a subordinate to self-actualise for them.)

GOODBYES

Conduct exit interviews with employees who leave the organization voluntarily. Ask them to give you a frank assessment of your strengths and weaknesses as a leader. Listen carefully to any personal criticism, however savage. Thank them for their frankness. As soon as they've left the room, run to the door, open it, and shout down the corridor after them, 'Well you're never going to get a reference from *me*, asshole!'

THE TEAM

A management team is like the cast of a big musical – you need a few stars, but you can't do it without the chorus. (And you don't have to pay the chorus much.)

TIME MANAGEMENT

If you have problems using your
time efficiently, keep a time-log.
Spend at least an hour a day keeping
it up to date.
Draw a daily pie-chart comparing your
ideal and your actual time allocations.
Form a time-management support group
which meets regularly every morning to
discuss and compare personal time-logs.
Hold end-of-day meetings where
time-flow charts and efficiency indices
are examined and discussed.
Go home and rest up.

MOTIVATION
#3

When something important needs doing,
don't just turn to a subordinate and say,
'do it'.
Instead, motivate and inspire by saying,
'do it or you're finished'.

A BAD MANAGER SAYS:

Look, I don't care whether you like it or not, if you fuckwits don't work harder for the same money, some guys in Tokyo will take their investment some place else, where there's no unions and people are happy to work for a dollar an hour, and then you won't have a job at all, will you, so shut the fuck up, okay!?

A GOOD MANAGER SAYS:

Globalisation.

A BAD MANAGER SAYS:

We're laying off 25 per cent of the workforce.

A GOOD MANAGER SAYS:

We're rightsizing the company.

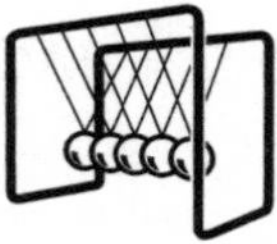

A BAD MANAGER SAYS:

You're going to have to work twice as hard for the same money.

A GOOD MANAGER SAYS:

We're introducing enhanced performance goals.

A BAD MANAGER SAYS:

I'm afraid we're sending you to our Bosnian office.

A GOOD MANAGER SAYS:

As part of a human resources redeployment programme, we're offering you an enhanced relocation opportunity.

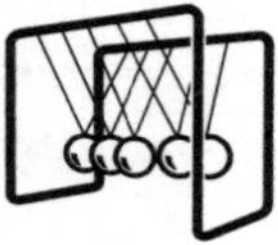

A BAD MANAGER SAYS:

Who cares if you don't like it,
it's going to happen.

A GOOD MANAGER SAYS:

Where an altered variable prompts negative feedback, forward system thinking on the part of management will result in a strengthening rather than a weakening of the inherent structural stability of the organisation.

A BAD MANAGER SAYS:

We'd like to involve staff more in the decision-making process, so that responsibility is shared. This means that if *we* get it wrong, *you* take the shit.

A GOOD MANAGER SAYS:

Empowerment.

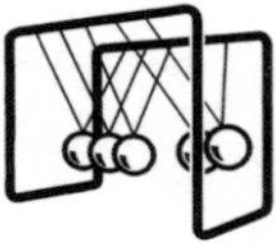

PRODUCT DEVELOPMENT

As a top manager, you are also a product.
Like a product, you need development.
Like a product, you need a profile.
Like a product, you need branding.
Like a product, you wear out and
need replacing.

(Don't think about the last one too much.)

DIVERSITY

Demonstrate your awareness of ethnic and religious diversity within your organization: cancel the Christmas bonus.

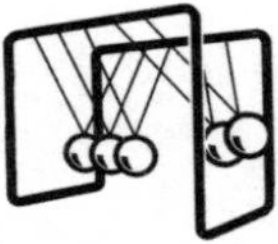

USEFUL ACRONYMS
3

Challenges
Rewards
Algorithms
Paradigms

THE KEY WITHIN

The key to solving most management problems is inside you.

If you can't solve a major problem, look for the key inside you.

(It is best to do this somewhere private.)

QUESTIONS MANAGERS ASK

Q: How do I know whether or not
I have emotional intelligence?

A: Push a subordinate out of an
18th floor window.
Ask yourself, 'How do I feel now?'
If you feel fine, you probably need
to do some more work on your
emotional intelligence

QUESTIONS MANAGERS ASK

Q: What's the best way of dealing with a colleague who's just been passed over for promotion?

A: When they greet you in the corridor, stop, stare, and ask in a puzzled tone, 'I'm sorry, do I know you?'

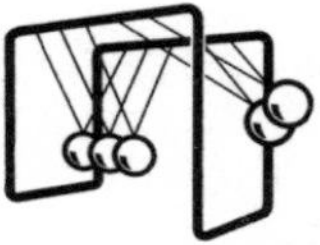

QUESTIONS MANAGERS ASK

Q: Do mission statements make a blind bit of difference?

A: This is an offensive question. Never, *ever* ask anybody this question.

QUESTIONS MANAGERS ASK

Q: What do I do if the CEO treats me with contempt?

A: Smile.

QUESTIONS MANAGERS ASK

Q: How do I push the envelope?

A: Don't. Get somebody else to push it for you.

QUESTIONS MANAGERS ASK

Q: A friend of mine went on a management course which ended with everyone having to walk across hot coals. What exactly does this teach you about being a manager?

A: It's a useful preparation for the office Christmas party.

ACTIONING CHANGE

As you fall asleep every night, ask yourself, 'how much change did I action today?' If the answer is, 'not enough', get out of bed again and action some change immediately. If you can't think of any change that needs actioning, go down to the kitchen and rearrange all the items in the fridge. When nobody can find anything at breakfast, invite family members to skip breakfast and instead take part in a discussion on the nature of change.

MULTI-SKILLING

Focusing on one single area of skills can be limiting. In the end you will become second-rate in your specialist area.

Multi-skilling can help you avoid this.

Why be crap at one thing when you can be crap at lots of things?

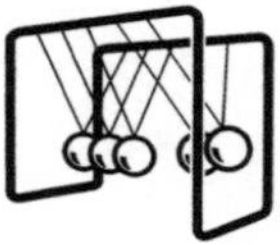

CAREER SETBACK

If you have a career setback, don't tell yourself you've been fired. Tell yourself you've been downsized or tell yourself you've been delayered or tell yourself you've been downshifted or tell yourself you've been re-engineered or tell yourself you've been repositioned. If that doesn't make you feel better, go to a bar, get drunk, and tell yourself you've been screwed.

CORE VALUES

The core values of an effective manager always reflect the core values of his or her employer. Should your own core values be different from your employer's core values, ask yourself, 'whose core values are more important, mine or my employer's?' If your answer is, 'well, mine, of course', then you urgently need to upgrade your core values.

DIFFICULT QUESTIONS

During important presentations, use humour to defuse difficult questions. For example, if somebody asks you something you can't answer, just smile and say:

'Hey, that's a tricky one – too tricky for me!'

or

'That's a very good question.
Wish I knew the answer!'

or

'Fuck off, smart-ass.'

MANAGING YOURSELF

You can't manage other people unless you know how to manage yourself.

Motivate and inspire yourself by means of classic management motivators (e.g., an enormous pay rise).

INTEGRITY

You cannot gain professional respect if your personal integrity is damaged.

Prevent damage to your personal integrity by leaving it at home in the mornings.

SHOWING YOU CARE

Show staff members you care by getting your secretary to send them bottles of wine for Christmas. Maintain a healthy competitive spirit by sending out different quality wines. When they thank you, say, 'Now remind me, did you get the case of best claret or the bottle of Bulgarian red?'

NEW RECRUITS

Make clear to new employees your personal commitment to a flexible, non-hierarchical, empowering and egalitarian workplace.

If they try to argue about that, tell them they can like it or lump it.

MULTICULTURAL COMPETENCE

In the modern global marketplace, multicultural competence is an essential management skill.

Enhance your multicultural competence skills by taking frequent foreign vacations.

DELEGATING

Don't delegate only routine or unrewarding tasks. Also delegate demanding, arduous and complex tasks (especially if you don't know how to do them yourself).

QUALITY FEEDBACK

When delegating tasks, always monitor and provide quality feedback. If the delegate performs badly, don't censure, because censuring demotivates. Instead, help the delegate reach a fuller understanding as to why they're a complete failure.

CHALLENGING ROUTINES

It's your job as manager to challenge
well-established routines.
Take a routine such as the lunch-break,
for example, and ask yourself:
Do employees really need a whole
hour for lunch?
Do employees really need to
leave the office for lunch?
Do employees really need lunch?

To develop these ideas further, invite a
senior colleague to discuss them over lunch.

WINNERS AND LOSERS

Never forget that a loser is only
a winner in disguise.

If you ever feel you're being treated like a
loser, just say to yourself,
'hey, maybe this disguise of mine
is too good!'

CONSENSUS

Harness the power of co-operation:
be a consensus builder.

- Create a motivational environment.
- Introduce an open-door policy.
- Foster a no-blame culture.
- Encourage reciprocity.
- Share your underwear.

SYNERGY

Team synergy sessions are the key to productive and effective mutual support systems.

Illustrate the power of synergy by getting everybody to lose their temper at the same time.

MILESTONE EVENTING

Mark important team successes by declaring them a Milestone Event. Milestone-event some of the following:

- A team member gets promotion.
- A new product is launched.
- One of your team makes their first million-pound sale.
- Your company's share price reaches a new high.
- Jerry in Accounts gets your expenses paid on time.

USEFUL ACRONYMS
#4

Generating
Revenue
Engenders
Executive
Delight

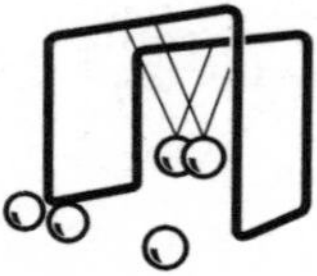

THE FIVE WHYS

Japanese business theory, or ***kan-do***, encourages employees to seek answers to *The Five Whys*:

1. Why does the customer buy our product?
2. Why am I committed to making our product even better?
3. Why is my company not yet the market leader?
4. Why do I believe in excellence at all levels of management?
5. Why has my life come to this?

SUGGESTIONS

A nervous manager will *never* ask a subordinate for suggestions.

A confident manager will *often* ask a subordinate for suggestions.

A wise manager will introduce a suggestions box and get a subordinate to open it.

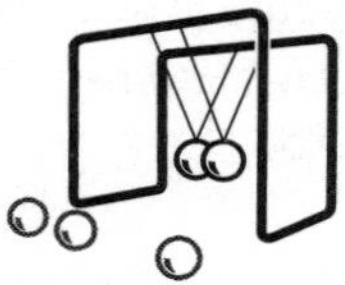

OUTSIDE CONSULTANTS

The arrival of outside consultants can sometimes stir up feelings of fear and resentment among staff, especially if the consultants are likely to recommend downsizing.

Ease fears by making sure the consultants' final report is completely incomprehensible.

(Most outside consultants will offer this service as a matter of course.)

EMOTIONAL LEAKAGE

Inappropriate emotional release is known
as *emotional leakage.*
Devise strategies to inhibit emotional leakage.
Next time you find yourself getting
emotional in a work situation, ask yourself,
'Am I relating or am I leaking?'

If you're not sure, you're probably leaking.

STRESS MANAGEMENT
#4

Sit down and make a list of 100 things that help you relax.

Don't give up until you've achieved all of them.

(Use best-value performance indicators to help you prioritise your relaxation needs.)

VIDEO-CONFERENCING

Optimize the chances of successful video-conferencing by wearing clothes.

RISK MANAGEMENT

In taking key risk management decisions, be sure to factor in possible exposure to discontinuities that can disrupt statistical prediction.

Such discontinuities might include:

- An earthquake in Tokyo.
- A comet landing on New York City.
- A meltdown at a European nuclear power station.
- A sudden rise in sea levels due to accelerating climate change.
- Getting stuck in the lift.

GROUP LOYALTY

Psychologists have ascertained that group loyalty is intensified and enhanced when members of the group truly love and respect one another.

Maximise the love and respect your team members feel for one another by making sure they never meet.

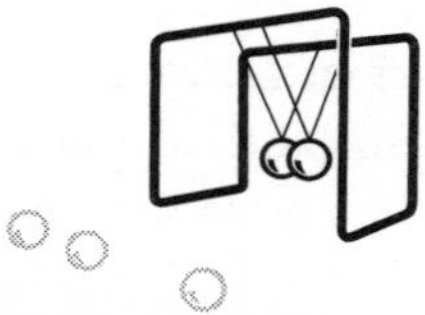

TRANSFORMATIONAL LEADERSHIP

Transformational leaders do more than just lead – they *transform* the world around them.
Christ was a transformational leader.
John F. Kennedy was a transformational leader.
Mother Teresa was a transformational leader.
Gandhi was a transformational leader.
Hitler was a transformational leader*.

*However, it is now generally acknowledged that Hitler lacked emotional intelligence, was poor at delegating, and sometimes failed to acknowledge the needs of others.

ARE YOU MICROMANAGING?

To check whether you're micromanaging, try this simple test:

Ask a subordinate to bring you a box of 500 paper clips.

If you count them, you're micromanaging.

IMPOSSIBLE

Impress on your team the power of positive thinking by banning the word *impossible* from group meetings.

If people go along with that, move on to banning the word *vacation*.

THE NATURAL ORDER

Organisations are living organisms.
They need to be given sustenance.
Management *is* that sustenance.
What the organism doesn't need is excreted.

Be needed.

PLEASURE

Every day do at least one thing that you enjoy:

- Go for a swim.
- Take a stroll in the park.
- Read a chapter of a book.
- Listen to some music.
- Drive over a pigeon on the way home.

KEEP UP TO DATE

Keep up to date with developments in the world of business, media, broadcasting and the arts, by clipping out important articles each day and filing them away by subject. At the end of twelve months, ask your secretary to read through the clippings and reduce the contents of the filing cabinet to a one-page précis (with bullet points).

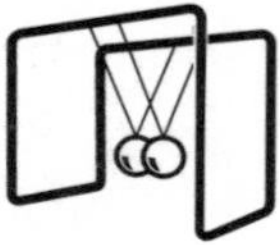

POSITIVE THINKING

There is no limit to the power of positive thinking.

(Well there is, actually, but you're a manager for God's sake).

ABOUT THE AUTHOR

Alistair Beaton lives globally and has seven habits, none of them highly effective.